Preface

This book is written based on my personal experience.

It is a story about the transformation of a little girl from an angry, introverted and unhappy person to an open-minded, kind and loving being. All it took was the love and support from one special person.

Not all kids are lucky to find that special someone in their lives. So I hope this book will illustrate a positive message to those who feel unaccepted. All that matters is how they feel about themselves. I wish they learn that it is important to be kind and love themselves. On the other hand, it is also written for children to recognize when their unhappy friends or classmates just need a little love and support.

I hope my readers feel the joy of seeing Flora transforming from "Flora in a funk" to "funky-happy Flora."

About the Author

I am a stay-at-home mother of two, an eleven-year old daughter and an eight-year old son. They are my heart and soul. I have brought them up to be good and kind persons. And they are. To me, they are the best kids! My goal as a parent is for them to have good lives and know how to be happy.

As a 46-year-old adult, I understand the importance of recognizing self-worth and feeling loved, especially for kids. Once loved, they learn to love, both others and themselves. It is the starting point of their path to happiness, peace and wisdom. I make sure my kids are cherished, praised and protected (but not over protected.) I hope that will prepare them for happy lives and a bright future.

Flora is in a funk! In fact, she has been in a funk for as long as she can remember. She does not like herself. She does not feel as beautiful as the others. Her petals are droopy and grayish. She does not smile. She feels as if she was an outsider and unaccepted. She is afraid to go in the crowd and socialize. She spends time by herself, looking out to the big world. It makes her feel lonely. All of these bad feelings make her sad and mad. She wishes her color was brighter, her petals would blossom and she could smile as big as sunshine.

Everyday, once the sun rises, everybody comes out to play. Their petals open up. They bloom and show off their bright and beautiful colors; yellow, orange, red, pink, purple… They hop, dance and run around. They have fun.

Flora can hear their laughter from far away. Flora wants to join in their fun, but she can't. She is not as pretty as them. She can only hide behind a tree and watch them enjoying the beautiful daylight. Sometimes she gets seen, but she still does not get invited to join them. "They just don't like me!" Flora thought.

Flora has her favorite spot to spend time alone. She sits on a log under a tree, up on the hill, looking down on the big green field. She watches everything happen. Birds fly across the sky, chirping. Butterflies land on flowers, drinking the nectar. Wind blows grass and flowers left and right, blowing leaves off the trees. The sun shines brightly, beaming warmth on her face. This is her place, where she feels safe and finds peace each day. Suddenly, on a particularly fine day, she is startled to hear "Hi!" And walking up behind her is a bright, yellow, bloomy, happy face.

"Hi, I'm Foster," he said. "What are you doing here all by yourself, all the time?" he asked. "Can I sit with you?"

Flora does not know what to think or say.

"What is your name?" he continued to question.

Taking a deep breath, she introduced herself and said "I'm here to do what I do everyday, just watch the world by myself."

"Why don't you go play with others?" he wondered.

"I am afraid nobody likes me. I am not as pretty and colorful as they are. And they never ask me to play with them either." Flora mumbled as she stared at the grass.

Surprised, Foster leaps up and says "Please come with me, Flora!"

Foster leads Flora onto the big green field where everyone is gathered. It is the first time she has ever been in the midst of all this activity, which she always watched from afar. It is strange, a little uneasy and overwhelming for her. Her heart starts beating faster and faster.

Foster stops Flora in front of two blooming faces.

"Fanny and Fred, this is Flora. Flora, these are my friends, Fanny and Fred."

"Hi Flora!" they beamed with a welcoming voice.

"Hi!" Flora replied meekly.

Foster introduces her to more of his friends, who have the big smiles on their faces. They are all happy to meet her.

"Oh no," Flora thinks, "I misunderstood them all this time!"

So what did she miss? Why did she have negative thoughts about them? Was it because she always closed herself up, hid away and only looked at things with anger? Was she just too busy feeling sorry for herself? Those who she thought did not like her were, in fact, nice to her. They accepted her and welcomed her as a friend.

Foster glimpses a little sparkle in Flora's eyes! It is an encouraging sign. This is a good start for Flora.

"Thank you for trusting me to take you to the field and introduce you to my friends, Flora!" Foster affirmed his appreciation.

"It was not as bad as you thought, right?" he continued. "There are good and bad things around us. It is really all about how you think and look at things. I choose to stay positive and see the bright side of the world. I just want to enjoy life at its best."

"You are one of our friends now. Please feel free to come and play with us at any time. It will make us happy!" He reminded her.

Flora tries to take everything in, "Thank you, Foster!" she replied.

The next morning, Flora comes to her usual spot, under the tree where she can see everyone down the hill. She remembers what Foster told her yesterday. She has made friends and she can go play with them. But she still feels intimidated. It is not easy for her to just walk up to them. She is not confident about herself. She decided she would rather stay behind the tree and watch them again today.

Then, Fanny and Fred arrive at the field and walk up to her.

"Hi Flora! Do you want to come play with us?" they ask enthusiastically and sweetly.

"Hi! Umm…yes, I will go play with you." Flora replies timidly.

Flora wakes up in the morning feeling tired the past few days. That is because she has been very active, playing with her new friends. She started with running around, up and down the hills. Then, she got to hop, skip and dance. It has been more and more fun each day. She loves this!

Today, Foster and Faith are teaching her to jump rope. She has been dreaming about doing it forever. She is super excited! Foster and Faith first take turns showing her how to do it. They, then, let her try. It takes a lot of coordination! She jumps slowly, much slower than them. Foster told her that was how he started. They both are patient. At the end of the morning, she is getting the hang of it. Now, it's break time. Pheww…. How fun!

Something is happening to Flora's petals. The two lower ones open up and bloom with bright beautiful color. It brightens her face, warms her heart and makes her smile. Everything looks more pleasant around her. The air smells fresher. The flowers seem to be sparkling while dancing in the sun with friendly butterflies.

"I feel happy!" Flora can't feel her feet on the ground. She can just float away with joy.

The past several days have brought her so many fun and happy moments. Each day, she replaces a past bad feeling with a good one. The empty space in her heart is getting smaller. She can feel the happiness inside and she knows it is the reason for the blooming. She can't wait for all of her petals to blossom!

Today is another beautiful day in the hills. Fanny and Fred are playing chase with Flora, while others are dancing around down the hill. Fanny and Fred want to show Flora a beautiful spot on top of the hill where they can see everything. It is such a fantastic sight.

Running back down the hill with her petals flowing back by the wind, Flora catches a glimpse of someone at the corner of her eyes. She has droopy and grayish petals. She is by herself. And she looks sad.

"Who is that?" Flora wondered. She never saw her before. "I don't know her but why do I feel like I know her?"

Flora feels such a sudden and strong connection with her. The reason is simply because she reminds Flora of herself.

Waking up this morning, two more of Flora's petals are blooming. She is ecstatic! She can't wait to show it to Foster and other friends.

"How wonderful, Flora! I am so happy for you." Foster expressed his excitement.

Flora feels elated! Besides the new found positive attitude she now has, she feels stronger. She is more confident. It gets easier each day for her to walk up and talk to her friends, play with them and have a good time. She finally gets to laugh. She also learns to be happy when she is by herself. She loves watching birds, butterflies and beautiful skies that constantly change into interesting shapes. She knows she has friends who love and care about her. And she loves them back.

For weeks, the image of the girl on the way down from the hill has stuck in Flora's mind.

"Where did she come from? Is she new around here? Or has she always been here? Where is she?..." Flora has so many questions. What she knows for certain is that the girl is in the sad place, the same place she had been before she met Foster.

Everyday, Flora looks for her. ...

"There she is!" Flora finally found her, down by the sea.

She collects herself and takes a deep breath before approaching her;

"Hi, I'm Flora," she said. "What are you doing here all by yourself?" she asked. "Can I sit with you?"